Dedication

To anyone who has navigated the muddy waters of divorce in any way...may you be able to relate even in some small way to the pages within. To my best friend, thanks for always being available for late night vent sessions and weekend getaways to heal my soul. To my parents, thanks for being the place of escape when I needed somewhere to go and for not disowning me. To my co-workers, thanks for keeping me grounded, and not constantly asking me how I was doing, but most of all for understanding that I needed to stay busy. To my kids, thank you for loving me through the fire even if you didn't understand it. To my ex, thanks for the lessons, now I know.

Lessons Learned:
Finding Grace Amid the Chaos of Divorce

Published by:
Powder River Publishing LLC
1014 Black Mountain Road
Thermopolis, Wyoming 82443

Copyright © 2022
ISBN: 978-1-956881-21-9
Printed in the United States of America

www.powderriverpublishing.com

Table of Contents

Preface

I'm writing to you as a single mom of two amazingly beautiful little girls! They keep me on my toes, humble, honest, and at times far too busy. But, I wouldn't have it any other way! While growing up, I never pictured myself with kids. They just weren't in my grand master plan. That plan included being some sort of a businesswoman who wore high heels and a pantsuit to work. However, as life would have it, my calling was actually teaching students language arts in the classroom. My bigger calling though, being a mom.

Never in a million years did being divorced enter the master plan either. But here I am, happier than I ever was while married. Please don't think that I condone getting a divorce, I don't. But I also do NOT believe living a life of misery is healthy for anyone involved. So, for what it's worth, huge lessons were learned during my first, and currently only, marriage. These lessons should have been common sense, but somehow got lost behind the mirage of perfection. It's my hope that reading this book helps someone feel validated and like they aren't crazy!

Chapter 1
Hurt People, Hurt People

Oddly enough, I had never really thought about this state-
ment until I was the one who made him hurt. I had two affairs on
my, now, ex-husband. The realization of what I had done to him
and the hurt I had caused him didn't really sink in until after I had
moved out. Because I had hurt him, he hurt me. He never physically hurt me, but verbally berated me and emotionally messed
with me for quite some time. He was on what I would describe as
an emotional roller coaster for months after I moved out. I didn't
file for divorce right away. In fact, we had been separated for six
months before I filed. One moment he would want to get back
together, the next he was yelling at me and scaring me to death.
On a few occasions he was so intimidating I almost called the
cops. This was his entire purpose. He wanted to scare me into not
leaving his hometown with the kids, even though I had no family
support there. He even threatened to get the court to prevent me
from moving altogether. Much to his dismay, that wasn't possible
because I wasn't planning on moving out of state. I was planning
on moving closer to where my family lived, so I could have a support system.

He made me believe I was crazy and should never have felt
the way I felt in our marriage prior to cheating on him. After all,
he was off making money. Don't get me wrong, because none of
what I'm about to discuss is an excuse for my actions. What I'm
saying is that our marriage was not an adequate marriage from
the start. From the time we started dating he worked a job that
required him to travel during the week. On top of being gone for
his "day job" during the week, he also is a basketball referee. This
means, that from the end of October to the middle of March he
graced us with his presence on Sunday only, long enough for me to
do his laundry. This routine of his worked for "us" until I had kids.
I didn't sign up to raise kids by myself. When my oldest was little

it was hard, really hard because not only was I working full time as a teacher, but I was also working on my master's degree. We had that conversation while I was pregnant and then again multiple times over the time span of ten years. The response was always the same, "I like my job, I'm not quitting". In all fairness to him, I never asked him to quit either job. I asked him to cut down on being gone so much so that he could be more present and help with the typical parenting gig. I was overwhelmed at home and at work. Several times over those years, while being completely overwhelmed with work and making things work by myself at home, I remember calling him sobbing on the phone. Only to hear, "I'm pulling up to my next house. I have to go". He is a traveling insurance salesman, who goes door to door. The lack of emotional support was exhausting to me. I needed someone to be there for me... physically and emotionally. To be blunt, he meant nothing to me at that point, except for the fact that he was the father of my children.

After years of having absolutely no emotional connection to my husband, feeling like I had no support (I don't mean financially), and feeling hurt because of this... I was DONE. In so many ways I was done. I was tired of not being taken seriously when I came to him with what I felt was a big enough issue to discuss. When I look back on the marriage, it was always his way. That isn't a marriage! Thus, the vicious cycle of the hurt, hurting the hurt. Lesson learned.

Chapter 2
Communication is the Life Line

Communication is vital to a relationship. I say "relationship" here instead of "marriage" because it doesn't matter if we are talking about a friendship, co-workers, a dating couple, or a married couple, this lesson applies to everyone in all walks of life.

During the first few years of our marriage, I didn't realize how very little we actually communicated verbally. We talked on the phone while he was away, but the conversation quickly turned to "how's the weather?" or "how are the kids?". We (yes, I included myself in this) often didn't listen to actually listen, but to respond. When he was home, we were intimate sometimes but then always went about our very different paths. But even sex felt forced and like it was a job. I look back and wish at the time I had known how truly important communication is to a relationship. Being able to read the ups/downs and highs/lows of someone just by analyzing their body language is valuable to any relationship, even if it's not an intimate one. Believe me when I say, even if a person doesn't come right out and bluntly tell you what's on their mind, if you are in tune and are paying attention enough to their body language, they will tell you (without telling you) how they are feeling. Verbal communication is vital, but so is being able to read someone's emotions. Thankfully, I've been lucky enough to have people teach me this in life after divorce.

Chapter 3
Your Time Means Everything to Someone

Nothing says "you are my top priority" better than giving that person your time and attention. This goes for all walks as well: kids, spouses, employees, and students. If you aren't present in that moment, the moment is lost. This is one of the hardest concepts to grasp because people are busy! Life is busy. Work is busy.

I often felt as though the girls and I weren't important to him because he didn't spend what I would call "quality time" with us. When he was home, he was taking care of things I didn't get accomplished while he was away. I held my own, but working full time and having two small kids at home didn't leave much free time to get all the extra honey-do items accomplished. He also purchased a trailer court (I was not on board with this idea) which took a lot of his time when he was home. Oh... I found out about said purchase when the title company called and left a voicemail letting him know when the closing was. How's that for lack of communication with your spouse? Yes, I was angry, beyond angry actually. Anyway, there was always something that needed to be done there. Often, he was cranky that he spent all week working to provide for the family, only to come home to do more. It was a brutal catch-22.

Sometimes we would do a fun family activity like dinner and a movie, or the swim park, or a 4-wheeler ride, but those times were few and far between. Simply being present when at home would have gone a long way. But instead, he spent those moments on his phone, scrolling through who knows what. And honestly, I'm just as much to blame here because after holding down the fort all week with the kiddos, when he was home, I needed a break. Even if that break meant going to Walmart for groceries by myself! I wasn't good at giving him my time. Sure there was the occasional date night, but neither one of us would sacrifice our phones to spend quality time with each other, heaven forbid we should miss out on something in the Facebook world!

A wise person once told me... "you want to FaceTime?", "then get in my face!" Be physically in front of me. I'm going to leave that there, as it needs no further explanation. Because of that conversation, I try really hard to be more present in the lives of the ones I love. Yes, it's hard sometimes because the phone is an awesome distraction from life. But, I would much rather strengthen the relationships I currently have with time spent living in the moment with those who are most important to me.

Chapter 4
Date Night Really is Important

Making time for your spouse or boyfriend/girlfriend is so important. The last chapter leads nicely into this topic. Once upon a time, I asked my grandparents who had been married for 50 years what the secret was to a long, happy marriage. Their answer without hesitation was to go on a date night every week. My grandma even mentioned how hard that was sometimes, especially with kids. Their date night was to go square dancing every Saturday night! They were an amazing couple who had the utmost respect for each other.

I think of the life I lived while married. There is no way we could have gone on a date night every week! He was gone most of the week, but even if he had been home... that would have been extremely hard to fit in. Then again, maybe that's why we are divorced. We didn't make time for one another. We didn't set aside a few hours a week to simply be with each other, to enjoy one another.

When he was home, he was tackling the honey-do list. The things I wasn't able to get accomplished while working full time and raising two tiny humans. Yup, looking back, I absolutely know this played a role in the demise of our marriage. Giving your partner your uninterrupted time for a date night is one of the most important factors in a marriage. Because this time is time spent actually enjoying the other person. More often than naught, the time we tend to spend together is time spent getting things done because we have to... like cooking, cleaning, mowing, feeding the animals, you get my point. Date night is special.

Chapter 5
Share the Chores

I feel like this one is pretty self-explanatory, but I'm going to mention it anyway. Guys, your wife was not put on this planet to simply have children, cook, and clean. Ladies, your man was not put on this planet to mow the yard and take care of the car. So often couples fall into the rut of the wife taking care of all the household chores. It gets super overwhelming to take care of small children and keep the house up. If you are trying to hold down a full-time job outside of the home (because God knows being a stay-at-home parent is a full-time job in itself) that chore becomes 10 times harder. So all I'm saying is, share the chore list! The list is long! We all know what's on it...

• Laundry
• Cooking
• Cleaning
• Grocery shopping
• Meal Planning
• Paying the bills
• Mowing
• Taking care of the kiddos (especially when they are little)
• Feeding the animals if you have them
• Honey-do-list

I'm sure you can add plenty to this list. This seemed like a pretty generic one to put here. It's not one person's job to do all of what is on the list.

I know that in my marriage because he was away so often, I felt like the list was all mine to tackle each week. Crossing everything off by the end of the week eventually became a goal I never reached. Year after year not feeling like I was accomplishing enough got old quickly. I realize he was gone for his job, but there were so many times when he was "working" but he was actually golfing with buddies or fishing. While I was at home taking care of what needed to be done. I was exhausted and burnt out!

If two people made the house/bought the house then the same two people should be taking care of the house and those in it. Just my opinion, but I think it would save a lot of frayed edges if the slack were picked up by the party that isn't pulling their weight.

Chapter 6
Let it Out

When going through a divorce, whether you want it or not, you might feel like you are the only one to ever go through this hell. Remember that you are not alone! Unfortunately, so many people have gone through this. It's also important to remember to let your emotions out. If you bottle everything up inside, it will come back to bite you eventually. Letting it out will look different for you than it did for me. I chose to ride my horse, go to the gym, clean... I cleaned a lot. My house has probably never been cleaner than it was when I was going through my divorce. The second he picked up the kids for his weekend, I started cleaning. Because if I didn't start doing something, the chances of my brain overthinking were pretty high. I always needed to be physically doing something. Idleness was evil when it came to my mental health.

Eventually, I started seeing a counselor because I felt like I was going crazy. I needed someone to tell me I was okay. I needed someone to confirm that I was truly not the only one to ever go through this. I needed someone to confirm that I was going to make it to the other side.

A few times, I broke down. And by "broke down" I mean I completely lost it, ugly cried my guts out. One time, in particular, my oldest daughter gave me a Mother's Day card she had made at school that year... She would have been 8 years old at the time. I read it and literally fell apart. It talked about some pretty raw and ugly stuff, and she was only 8 years old (my youngest was only 4 at the time). No kid should have to even think about the hard stuff like that. At that time we had been separated since August, but I had only filed a few months before, so things were still raw. We hadn't even settled on everything yet. I always felt like being a mom, that I needed to hold it all together, to be strong for my kids. But what I learned from all that was, that it's okay to let it out. It's okay to let your kids see you being human! Looking back now, I think it would have been really sad had they not seen my break down. I want my daughters to know that showing emotion is a completely normal thing to do, especially when you are hurting. With that being said, for the most part I held myself together, but there were a few times that I simply couldn't, and it was okay.

Chapter 7
Your Kids Will Thrive

Four years ago, if you would have told me that my kids were going to be okay through all of this, I would have thought you were crazy! I held a lot of guilt because I put my kids through a divorce. I'm the one who left their dad. I could have stayed unhappily married to their father forever. But we were in a loveless marriage, and I felt as though letting them grow up to believe that a lack of affection was normal, was worse than putting them through a broken family. But when people would tell me "your kids will be okay", it made it worse. Because I didn't just want my kids to be okay, I wanted them to thrive.

For the first year of our separation helping the kids through the chaos was really hard. He would come over, because boundaries weren't a thing for him, even though I had moved into a rental in town. He would come over and no matter how many times he said he didn't want to fight, he would pick a fight and yell and scream at me. He would always end up crying. By that time my cry-o-meter was broken around him. But he would always cry, and the girls saw that and when he would leave they would ask me why I always made daddy cry. That was HARD! I wasn't trying to make their daddy cry. I was simply trying to move forward. But they were much too little to understand the painful process of divorce.

From the moment I moved out, we kept the kids on the schedule of what I knew the court would rule. I knew that because their father works on the road and isn't home to care for them during the week. So I figured it would be every other weekend with their dad... alternating holidays. I opted to not have them the first Christmas because I just wanted to get it out of the way. They were okay. I was NOT. I cried all day, and I spent the day by myself. I didn't go anywhere. My parents were in Arizona, I was in Wyoming. My best friend was in Montana. I had plenty of invitations, but I was in no mood to be around anyone and didn't want to bring anyone else's day down. So I stayed home and cried. It sucked. I did get to see them for a bit and that made it easier, but that first holiday away from the kids will rock your world in the worst kind of way. But they were so strong!

I have always admired their strength. Honestly, they got me through the tough days. I would come home from work, hug them and be okay. We got into a routine after divorce, the three of us. We are pretty tight because of it. Every night we say prayers, read a devotional if we have the time, and that has kept us going.

To say my kids haven't struggled would be a lie. But I'm telling you, they have seen the difference between a miserable mom and a happy one. They would pick the happy one all day long, even if it meant their dad wasn't in the picture full-time. For us, he was never in the picture during the weeks anyway, so this really wasn't much of a change. They have now been in the current school they are in for the same amount of time they were in the school that we left when we moved. They have amazing friends, an amazing support system, and an amazing community to lift them up.

My oldest daughter is now 11 years old and is involved in everything! Literally, this year I told her she can't be involved in any more activities that are outside my work hours (I work at the school too) until she has her own driver's license! She does piano lessons, Student Council, Food Group, Recycling Club, and basketball. My youngest (she's only in 1st grade) did the fall and spring seasons of soccer this year and wants to start piano lessons next year. They are both thriving in their worlds. Every day they amaze me with their strength, resilience, and love!

Please don't think that I don't realize there could still be issues that arise in the future with the girls that stem from the divorce. I know. I'm prepared to deal with issues as they come up. Until then, I'm going to relish the fact that my kids are happy and healthy... even after the divorce!

Chapter 8
Top Priority

Never settle for someone whose priorities aren't where they need to be! This one is quite touchy for most, myself included. Since meeting my ex, he has been a basketball referee. That meant that from the end of October to the middle of March the weekends were tied up with games and him being essentially absent from our lives (I may have already mentioned this). He also traveled for his work during the week. So you can do the math here... It's one thing that I wasn't one of his top priorities, but it's a whole other monster that his kids weren't his top priority!! This was something that we had talked about many times from the time I found out I was expecting because I didn't want to raise my children alone. It had come up so many times, each time with the same outcome. He would tell me that he liked his job and wasn't willing to find something closer to home that meant he could be around more.

Since being divorced he has proven what his top priorities are over and over again. This makes me sad on a level I can't even explain to you. Because without me saying anything to the girls about it, they have picked up on it. It breaks my heart to see their disappointment in their dad. He gets the girls every other weekend during the school year. In the last 3 years, there have been so many weekends where he has simply said he wouldn't be getting them because of reffing or something has come up. For example, this coming weekend... he will be at a reffing camp in Las Vegas. Of course, he didn't bother to communicate that with me until a few days ago. The girls miss their dad even though they don't say that very often. But my biggest concern for them is that they will grow up with a complex thinking they aren't good enough for him. That they aren't important enough. That their events/activities aren't what's important to their dad. That part is heartbreaking to me and there is nothing I can do about it, other than be there to support my kids in any way I can.

Chapter 9
Take You Time
Seriously

As a single mom, I go between craving time to myself and feeling guilty about taking time for myself! It's a constant battle. But know this... taking time for yourself means that you will be a better mom, teacher, friend, co-worker, and girlfriend... It's so important to be able to process how your life has changed, and what you plan to do about it.

That TIME to yourself will look different for everyone, and that's okay. But do yourself a favor and take it! You might be someone who gets up early to have some quiet time that includes just you and the Bible. You might be someone who likes to go for a walk every day or a run. Maybe you want to go to the gym and work out or go for a horseback ride. It doesn't matter what the time looks like, just take it. Make a point and don't feel guilty about it. Being the best version of yourself is important! It's also important to those around you!

Chapter 10
Don't Quit Your Hobbies

You are likely the person you are partly because of the activities you love to do. Right? For example, if you love horseback riding and own horses you probably have some qualities such as: being responsible, strong work ethic, grit, compassion, patience, and probably broke! That last one is a joke, kinda. But seriously, what you love to do has a way of shaping you into the person you are today.

So don't get married and then lose that awesome person you are. Do the things you love to do still. Make time for them. If you don't make time for the hobbies that you love to do, you will lose who you are. Eventually, you won't like who you are anymore. Believe me, it takes time to get back to those roots when lost.

Chapter 11
Never Settle

Oh my gosh! Once you go through a divorce you become slightly picky about what you expect in your future partner. Slightly might not be the right term, you become extremely picky because you know exactly what you DON'T want now. You know what you never want to go through again. That's a scary place to be because somewhere in the middle of a failed relationship, you lose faith in your ability to make good choices where the relationship is concerned.

This is what I've learned about not settling. Dating after divorce is hard! First of all, what dating looked like 20 years ago, and what it looks like now are different. Holy cow! But also, if you have kids then there's always the dilemma of whether or not to introduce them to the new man in your life. When is the right time for that? All of these questions and issues arise when dating after divorce. My advice is simply to not settle. If there are red flags, be honest with the other person and communicate what those flags are. But in the end, if it's not going to work, let them go.

The relationships that you are in after divorce will teach you things about yourself ! It helped me to let go of the pain and hurt from my failed marriage. I learned to let go of the stress, I learned to be honest with myself, and I learned that you can trust someone again with your emotions.

For quite a while after divorce you live in a state of constant trauma, it's the fight or flight response. It wreaks havoc on your heart, body, and mind. So, although you may want to jump right into another relationship, it probably won't work out simply because you are still trying to get over the things that happened in the past relationship. It's not an easy process and it takes time. In the meantime, enjoy yourself, and your kids and take the time you need to heal. When the time comes to date again, don't settle for anything less than you deserve!

Chapter 12
It's OK to not be OK!

There will be times that you are not going to be ok! People will ask you often how you are feeling and 9 times out of 10 you are going to say "I'm doing ok". But in reality you are a hot mess!

There were times during that process I felt like I was the only one in the world to ever go through a divorce. I knew, of course, that I wasn't, but that doesn't change the fact that I felt super alone.

There are moments that you are going to feel completely confident in your decision. There are moments you are going to question every single thing you are doing. This roller coaster of emotions makes the process much harder to navigate. Remember though, that you won't feel alright all the time which is completely normal.

If you did, I would be worried! Because even if the divorce is what you wanted, it sucks and it's hard and it brings out the worst of all parties involved. So it's okay to not be okay!

Chapter 13
Honesty is the Best Policy

This is absolutely the most steadfast advice that my parents taught me growing up. I sure wish I had followed it from the beginning with my ex. There came a point in our relationship where we stopped communicating entirely. We just lived our lives without talking to one another about anything other than the kids and the weather. So until I felt ready to actually make a change, I kept quiet about my infidelity. When I knew I was ready to leave I fessed up. Please don't think that I believe this was the best option. I do not, and if I had it to do over, I would have approached that much differently.

There were plenty of times in our marriage when he wasn't honest with me as well. So many times after a long week of working and raising our two kids while he was supposed to be at work, he would say he had another appointment and would be late getting home that week. On lots of occasions he wasn't actually working, he was golfing with buddies, or at an auction, or simply just watching basketball. It was crushing to me because that isn't what he told me.

One time in particular we had a voicemail left on our home phone. It was a local title company about a closing date on a trailer court. We had discussed this purchase six months earlier one time and I had expressed my dislike for many reasons. This purchase was a family deal, but because he was already gone so much, I knew that this would mean when he was home, he would be taking care of the trailer court instead of spending time with us. This was the main reason why I was against the purchase. I have never been so mad in my life as I was that day. Thinking back on it I know that he chose to not be honest with me because he knew it would be a fight.

There were a million times that he and his dad would go to an auction and buy guns and then lie to their wives about who actually bought it. I caught both of them in that lie too many times to count.

Had both of us followed the infamous advice of honesty is the best policy throughout the years of our marriage, we might have at least been friends. We weren't even that.

You guys (or gals), whoever is reading this, please be honest with your partner. Since ending my marriage and having adultery under my belt (or burned on my forehead like a scarlet letter), I have made myself a promise... before getting into a serious relationship with someone, I owe them the simple truth about my past. Anyone who decides to be in a serious relationship with me will know about the choices I made. Otherwise, I would feel like my relationship started off with dishonesty and I don't feel like that's the best way to begin what could be forever. Yes, I'm open to that again, someday.

Chapter 14
Give Grace

This... so much this! I, like most women, am really hard on myself. The thoughts that crossed my mind, sometimes still do, are not the most forgiving. When I think about women being hard on themselves, the number one factor that comes to mind is their appearance or weight. Well, during divorce, that was not a problem for me because I rarely ate, worked out, and wasn't healthy. When I'm stressed, I don't turn to food, I turn away from it. I still ate, just not much. I had absolutely no appetite and only ate because I knew I needed to. What I learned from that is that you have to give yourself a little grace. Each person handles stress differently and it's probably alright as long as it doesn't become dangerous.

I was also really hard on myself because I could have made some different decisions in my life. I could have not had 2 affairs. I could have communicated more, I could have tried harder, I could have been more supportive of his career, I could have done this and I could have done that. I was my own worst critic, most people are. What I should have realized was that what was done was done. I needed to simply make better choices, learn from my mistakes, give myself some grace, and move onward.

My kids needed some grace too! Bless their little hearts, they stumbled through the whole mess like little rock stars! I seriously can't even believe how amazing they did, but there were times that they too needed a little extra love and comfort. They were trying to navigate an adult issue as little girls. Sometimes they just needed an extra hug, support from adults who weren't their parents, and a hobby to turn to to keep their minds from overthinking. Honestly, that was no different than me. I needed all those things too.

So, giving yourself and those close to you some grace especially through the hard times is super important. You won't regret that at all, in fact... that will be a huge relationship builder for you and your loved ones.

Chapter 15
It Does Not Matter
What People Think!!

The most important lesson I learned was not to care about what others think. It's so hard not to worry about what others think of you when going through a divorce. Unfortunately, we live in a world consumed by what others think. I'm going to be brutally honest here, you can't give a shit about what others think, because if you do it will ruin you. It is natural for that to be an initial reaction, but you will quickly determine that it doesn't matter. I think my failed marriage was the hot topic of the town for about a month until something else more riveting came up. The fact that people can't just keep their noses out of the business of others is sad but so completely true. At the time it angered me but mostly made me even sadder. Because there was so much more than they even knew going on... and had been going on for years. Yet, they were only concerned with the outcome.

That particular experience has shaped me into who I am today. I live my life how I want to live my life. I don't need the approval or acceptance from others to do so. How I wish that I had learned that lesson prior to my divorce... things would have been so much easier! Not uncommon though, I felt that I had a reputation to uphold. The "perfect family" sticker to boldly display on my car window. But all that was fake, and I got really tired of living a false life.

Chapter 16
Move On

Holy cow! Even if you are the one who wants out of the marriage, moving on can be difficult. I mean 2, 5, 14, 20 years is a long time to be with someone. Regardless of how happy or unhappy you were, change is hard. I wanted nothing more than to move on, but I'm not going to lie and tell you it was an easy process. I felt like I was stuck. Stuck in some sort of unknown hell. The element of the unknown is so hard for me. Maybe for some, it's not debilitating, but for me it is. I have to have some resemblance of control in my life, or at least feel like I do.

To start with, I decided to separate and move out for a bit. Not because I wanted to rehabilitate my marriage, but because I thought it would buy some time for his emotions to calm down a bit. In hindsight, that was a dumb idea. Dumb because I think it left him with the hope we would get back together. Honestly, I never wanted that, and I don't truly think he did either, but he didn't want to go through a second divorce. Looking back, I should have just filed the day I moved out. I think it would have prevented at least some of the nasty unknown I'm referring to. I also believe it would have made moving on easier to an extent. There at least would have been no guessing at the next angle.

I was dating before my divorce was final. In all honesty, it was with the guy who I had the second affair with. But none of that was fair to him or me. It was way too hard to try to have a serious relationship with anyone while in the midst of a divorce. He often wondered why things weren't moving faster with paperwork on my end and I didn't want to be pushed at all. I did what I did because at the time I felt like it was the best option for all involved. We felt like we snuck around a lot, not wanting to make waves with my soon to be ex-husband. None of it was conducive to building a strong, long-lasting relationship for sure.

When the time is right for you though, do move on. And do so with confidence. If you are still reading this, you have waited too long to be happy. So go for it. Don't second guess yourself, don't self-sabotage, have fun, and don't look back. You can absolutely find happiness in your life. I 100% believe it exists, and you should too!

Chapter 17
Red Flags

Going through a divorce will make you very picky pertaining to potential life partners. It will make the "red flags" in everyone stand out like a flashing caution light. I think you are more aware of your own red flags too.

Recently, I had a particular incident occur and I can remember the mental alarm going off in my head warning me of the meteor size red flag that had just waved right in front of my face. In this incident I had been spoken to like no one should be spoken to for any reason. My first instinct was to run. Not because I was scared, but because I was mad and I wanted to enjoy my evening and not have to fake it with anyone. But I figured that probably wasn't the most adult way to face the problem, so I didn't. You can bet however that I didn't let it slide. In my past relationships, I would have simply gotten super quiet (by the way…. If a woman gets quiet, things aren't good), and swept my feelings under the rug just like the million others that had been placed there. You and I both know how that turned out, so I didn't go there this time. We had to have a pretty difficult conversation on why the way I was spoken to wasn't okay. Why that is nonnegotiable for me and should it happen again, I'm walking. Nothing about the whole ordeal was comfortable, in fact, it was on the painful side. But I gave myself some kudos for standing up for myself and how I deserve to be treated.

If you have kids, it doesn't matter if they are male or female, ask yourself this question: Would you want your son/daughter to be spoken to in that manner? If the answer is no, then something needs to be done about it. Here is a simple truth… your children are watching what you put up with. So give yourself the green light to be picky. When red flags occur, deal with them if you think it was a one time thing, or walk away.

After my divorce I learned what I do not want in a man. I learned what I do not want in myself. I learned what I do not want for my kids. So, it's my job to make sure those things on the DO NOT WANT list never enter my life again, which is why I'm going to listen when the "red flag" warning alarm goes off in my head.

Chapter 18
If It Won't Matter in Five Years, Let it Go

At times I look back on my marriage, especially in the early years of realizing there were so many times when I should have let things go. There were lots of little things that really didn't matter at the time, but I was too young and immature to know that at the time. I can remember being so mad at him sometimes. It wasn't until the later years that I realized that those were piddly things.

They absolutely should not have been taking up space in my mind at that moment. However, the part that really sunk in for me was the fact that there were major things that would matter five years down the road that didn't get enough of my attention. Some things I went along with simply because I hated conflict. I still hate conflict but I do know now when I need to speak up.

I just recently started talking to my oldest daughter about this concept. I want her to understand that in life it's okay to let the small things go. But it's not okay to let the bigger things go. If it's going to impact you down the road then it's worth a pretty serious conversation.

Where we failed in our marriage was either not having the big conversations at all or having them but to no avail. More often than not, we had a hard conversation, but if he wanted to do it, then it didn't matter what my opinion on the matter was. Don't get yourself into the situation, ever. If your opinion doesn't matter to him, take a serious look at the relationship you are in. Your opinion should matter to whoever you are with.

Chapter 19
Take Ownership

It's okay to own your shit! Please do own it. I wish more people would. In the past, I've made mistakes, but I've also owned them. My ex couldn't own up to anything that might have been his fault. He simply couldn't do it, because he felt like it would ruin his pristine reputation with his friends and family. Well, the news is, that he is likely to continue to never own up to anything he does wrong in a relationship. That's okay because he's somebody else's problem now.

If you are willing to own your mistakes, the next person is going to have a lot more respect for you. On the flip side of that, you are going to be able to move forward faster and not remain hung up on the past. Owning your crap isn't easy to do, but it's a necessary evil in order to move on in life and feel good about being in your own skin.

Chapter 20
Tougher Than You Think

If you are a country music fan, Chris Ledoux probably said it best when he wrote the song "Tougher Than the Rest".

But that phrase goes so much deeper in the world of getting a divorce. If you are about to go through a divorce you are soon going to realize that you are absolutely tougher than you think you are.

You will go through emotions that will feel unsurvivable. You will feel like certain phases are never going to end. I remember wondering if I was ever going to feel emotionally stable ever again. There are days you are going to feel like you are drowning and no one is coming to your rescue. If you are the one choosing to leave, there will be times when you are going to question your decision.

Emotions run extremely high during this time. For me, there was a very brief time with I questioned my decision to leave. But it was only to protect my children from what I knew would rock their world. I didn't want to stay. I didn't want to be in the same loveless situation 10 years down the road. I made the decision to not look back. That doesn't mean that when he started seeing someone else I didn't have some weird emotions about it.

I didn't want him and I knew that. But it was still really odd when he started seeing someone else. He tried so many times to get back together even after he was seeing someone, which was messed up on so many levels. It all scrambled my emotions.

I just wanted to be done with all of it. I didn't start to feel "normal" if you will until I moved several hours away and started my new chapter in life. To give you a timeline of how many months I was out of sorts... 1 year. I said I wanted a divorce in June, moved out of the house (but stayed in the same town) in August, filed for divorce in March, moved closer to home in June, my divorce was final in July of the following year.

Honestly, when I look back at the process it doens't really

seem like it took that long. When I was in the middle of all of it though, it felt like it would never end. I understand feeling completely helpless. But I'm pretty proud of the fact that my kids are doing just fine. I pay the bills by myself, I mow the lawn and take care of all things at my house by myself. I manage the practices, games, jobs... all of it on my own. I'm doing okay. Some days are harder than others, but that's true for everyone. I made it through. You will too.

Remember you are not the only person to ever go through a divorce, even if it feels like you are. Remember emotions will run high and that's normal too. Remember that lawyers take time!! That little tidbit is super frustrating. Remember to get along in front of your kids (I wish we had done that)! Remember to breathe. Remember to take time for yourself. Remember to take care of yourself. When it's all over you are going to look back and say I was tougher than I thought!

Powder River Publishing

www.powderriverpublishing.com

About the Author

Jae C. Royce was born and raised in the great state of Wyoming, where she still calls home to this day.

She has two daughters who are active in all sorts of school activities and sports, which keeps her active, engaged and always on the move.

Royce relishes spending as much time with her family as possible, attending her daughters events as their biggest cheerleader.

For the past 15 years Royce has served as an educator, working with youth ages 13-19.

Royce lives in a small Wyoming town in the shadows of the Rocky Mountains.

www.ingramcontent.com/pod-product-compliance
Lightning Source LLC
Chambersburg PA
CBHW061329120626
46546CB00007B/2732